Unstarted

Poems by Chris Michaels

Table of Contents

Part One - In Bed

Part Two - She

Part Three - Unstarted

Table of Contents

Part Four - Goodbyes

Part Five - Tomorrows

Part One - In Bed

skeletons

The skeletons in
my closet aren't
skeletons yet.

Their skin is still soft,
their muscles tough,
their eyes judging.

They shout from inside,
louder than the clock
louder than the radio,

but only I can hear them.

comfort

Comfort can go unnoticed
until its gone — broken.

Nights of sweat
on top of sheets
fewer clothes.

Sore ankles, sore arches.
Sore eyes, sore ears.

Scratchy sweaters and
noisy windows,
they point out comfort's absence.

Comfort is hard to
celebrate when it's
hard to notice.

like water to a fish
only when it flounders and gasps.

And oh, do I flounder and gasp.

overnight storage

My bedroom is overnight storage
for my laundry, clean and dirty,
for my linens and my sheets,
vital documents and precious memories,
but most importantly,

my bedroom is overnight storage
for me.

lighter

I'm never lighter than just before
I get out of the bath and
the weight of my body comes
rushing back.

smothering

It is me.

I've spent my life
convincing myself
that to be true.

It smothers me
with every turn.
Every heave.
Every bend.
Every way.

My body, alone
in its bed.

Its weight surprises me
its presence suddenly reminding.

I'm sorry, I can not sleep.
My body is smothering me.

sensitive

My body's sensitive,
it hurts and makes weak.

My shoulders ache,
stiff in my spine.

My tongue burns,
dainty to coffee and tea.

My heart beats fast,
longing for those who
will never be mine.

one bedroom

Home alone, in a
one bedroom
when I know they're out.

She's telling a story,
he's sipping his drink,

he makes a joke about him,
she openly flirts with her,

natural and common,
what normally happens at
places like these, at
times like this, to
people like them.

Back and forth,
their volley keeps up
while I'm home alone
in my one bedroom.

sunrise

I don't see the romance
in my simple actions
like I do in you.

The smallest gaze or
the quietest pause
causes me to swoon
when you do it.

The image of you
sitting up, back hunched,
at the end of your bed,
hair messy, sheets tossed,
watching the sun rise
in the wrong direction.

The street and the trees
and the sky slowly brightening
by a hidden source
behind your aged wooden house.

When it's you,
it's poetry as life.

When it's me,
I should go back to bed.

Part Two - She

tug at my heartstrings

I need to tug at
my heartstrings.

Be at beck and call
to my every word.

Hold my mind as a
thin thread between
my fingers, ready to
knot or snap at will.

Plunge my night
into darkness with
one sour tone in
my voice.

Fill me with hate or
bliss by the consequence
of myself,

the way you do to me.

bedfellows

With each session,
no matter how close
or how closed,
my other self
appears in your mind.

My guilt and
your inability to end this
make for
unwelcome bedfellows,
but fellows we have become.

bewitched

Her bewitching eyes,
full lips speak wonders,
thoughts distant and kind.

She casts a spell
with her gaze,
the innocent and
knowing giggle,
surpassing age
and grace.

to whom

To whom am I
what you are to me?

my fears grew

My fears grew
fears of their own.

Her secrets grew lies
designed to stomp me out.

My curiosity made me
lose trust and faith.

Her truth is better
than her.

My truth would forever
drive her away.

Ours is not to last
past our own fears.

in the way

In a kiss
lips get all the credit.

Noses and cheeks,
cheeks and chins,
fingers on chins,
on hips, on cheeks.

Eyes flickering open
to make sure
it doesn't end.

Lips feel like they're
in the way,
keeping us apart.

they've noticed

There is a shameful hope
which creeps into the mind
when things are going wrong.

The hope that it will pass
without needing anyone else.

The confident drive to
push through without showing.

The strength to handle it
all on my own.

Always denying. Always hiding.
Desperately running from
the embarrassment of being.

And that hope,
optimistic and selfish,
is gone all at once
when I'm on the floor
staring her in the eyes,
her hands on my cheeks.

This is a problem.
This is real.
This isn't going away.
They've noticed.

This is a problem.
Now *she*'s the one
telling me
"You'll be okay," instead.

Hope — telling me
not to worry, but
Honesty — wants me
to ask for help.

I tell myself
it will be okay.
But they've noticed and
I'm not on my own anymore.

fear

Fear is often said to be
heart-racing.

But so is running a mile
or having sex
or carrying moving boxes up
your new four story walk-up
in the big city.

Fear can also be
heart-stopping.

Worry, without heavy breaths

The feeling of slipping away
between two heart beats
that were just a little
too far apart.

it wasn't for me

It wasn't for me.

No, not the world.

Big business, courts and laws,
academia, soup kitchens, churches.

They were made for me,
almost to a tee.

Walking alone at night.
Haggling with the mechanic.
Mingling with road crews.
With sailors and soldiers.
These were made for me.

But that smile, just there…
That embarrassed, flirty smile…
That wasn't for me.

The joke to the table, somehow,
wasn't for me.
And somehow, we all knew it.

The flutter in your voice
was for him and him alone.

Nothing made for me compares.

(between the lines)

If it could have been
a different time,
we could have been
something different.

Part Three - Unstarted

sommelier of love

I am, myself, new to love.
The variety of flavors,
the enticing interactions.
They're foreign to me as
Algonquin to Zulu.

A sly wink.
An amorous hug.
Showing up, even though
they only said "maybe".

Love is more
than kissing, than fucking
than wedding bands
and family photo albums.

I am not a true
sommelier of love.
They all taste the same.
The notes still blur.
But now I'm starting
to separate my
reds from my whites.
I'm tasting for the
flavors of love I love.

baited breath

I'm waiting on you,
my baited breath,
to finish a thought
no longer relevant.

how do you love?

How do you love other people?
They're living their own lives.
Isn't it selfish to stop them to say,

"Excuse me, there's something
of a hole inside of me.
Would you mind taking up a
bit of its space?

I see you're getting on
fine without me, but
if you have any chores
or household errands,
maybe that will repay you
for making me feel like
a real person for
the first time in my life."

How do they not run?
Run away screaming?
Slap me across the cheek
and ask me how I
can live with myself.

I wonder how they
live with themselves.

catch up

My life is only just starting.
Your history is rich and long.

While I'm struggling to find
who I am.
You already know exactly
who you're not.

My life lacks the memories
that makes yours feel whole.

And as I desperately try
to catch up,
you're already over it all.
Just in time.

someone else's love

Can you discover yourself
in the desires of
someone else?

How can you tell
the difference between
your new authentic self™

and trying to be the man
she would love?

laundromat I

Guarding a single washer
with my upturned hamper
and a can of coke
from the machine.

I do what I can
to keep out of your way
as you tend to your flock
of washers and dryers
like a farmer checking on
the chickens in the morn.

Childish and pesky,
I must seem.
My small, clumsy load
compared to your
fleet of flannels
towers of towels
platoons of panties.

Looking longer
at your abundant piles
you seem susceptible
to skipping a week.
It's no wonder our paths
had, until now, steered clear.

unstarted

Trapped in an unstarted life.
Not stopped. Not interrupted.
But never started in the first place.

Going through the motions,
eyes stuck behind windows,
shut and locked tight.

An unexamined life is
not worth living.

An unstarted life doesn't
know what it's missing.

laundromat II

You're smart.
This isn't your first time.
You watch the timers.
Your carts and baskets
poised at the ready.

You're the type
who folds everything,
even towels,
before leaving.
What can't you handle?
What can't you handle?

not-good-enough

Faking (Experimenting)
Pure (Untouched)
Unfinished (Unstarted)

Real requires history.
My body has none.
Only imaginary scars,
cut by not-good-enough problems.

laundromat III

Chores aren't chores yet.
For me, they're still an
act of independence.
A chance to prove
I can take care of myself.

Chores are chores for you.
Maybe they always were.
Never having the luxury
of someone else taking
care of your every need.

You never got
to play pretend.
Make believe you were
okay on your own.
You had to keep the
plates spinning, never
stopping to question it.

I spent my life wondering
what it would be like
when I got to be you.

as much

With each passing year
I discover I am as much
my father's son as I am
my mother's daughter.

And yet,
neither see themselves in me.

layers I

Layers are how I know
I'm dressed for the weather.

The coat for rain and tears.
The sweater to keep me
warm and held.

The button down shirt says
I'm still trying.
Even when giving up
is only a button snap away.

The t-shirt underneath
is only for me.
I'm going to need
company in bed.

the christening

I am old, but not yet christened.
Alone on these open waters.
I sail along, my sea glistened
but in my head, I am sinking.

From what I have wrought,
alone I sail, yet not free.
I fear that the thought
consumes too much of me.

And after, whenever that is,
I might be more broken,
more lost, more empty
than I am now.

Lost at sea, your loss of self
swept up in every wave.
To go out with a whimper,
instead of the bang you crave.

you've forgotten

You've forgotten,
this has happened before.
You've forgotten,
their names, their lives.
You've forgotten,
the betrayal and heartbreak.

But what you haven't forgotten
is the lesson you learned
with each and ever one;

It won't end any different
unless you make a change.

Part Four - Goodbyes

things forgotten

The destruction of
things forgotten
weighs a painfully
light load.

I wear your face

I wear your face
upon my own
in my mind,
only to be disappointed
when I catch my
own reflection and
you vanish from my life again.

hole

I thought the hardest part
would be keeping my mind
off of you.

Instead,
the spots I hold painfully in
my head are empty,
gaping holes where
you once sat.

I don't think of you,
but I can't help stare
at the holes you left behind.

the globe in a pitch black room

The end is always worse
when you know it's here.

Finishing without shouting
but with a sad, apathetic fade
that blurs the lines between
love and sorrow decayed.

The new year brings,
after sorrow,
whatever comes next.

laundromat X

Suddenly the dryer bursts,
flames from beneath.
The alarms don't sound,
the TVs just play repeats.

I drive away,
light from behind
swelling in the sky.

Blackened quarters
and melted glass.

I fold, just this once.

always quiet

Breaking up can be loud.

Falling out of love is always quiet.

oh, let Seattle fade

Oh, let Seattle fade.
Its fog and rain mask.
Puget sound wash it clean.

Let Michigan melt.
Its oaks and brick
still in the Silver Harbor.

Let Korea surpass
my homeland, just like
its other battlefields before.

Enough of me lives in her brain
to get caught in her thoughts
as she does mine.

Let our life drift into her's
every now and again
as it does mine.

And let her learn
to live with herself

and without me.

learning moment

I've slipped up,
but you won't tell me
what I've done wrong.

This isn't a learning moment.
No chance to get better.
You saw me fall, and
you want me to keep falling.

Falling and falling,
because then you'll always be right.
Now, and next time.

grow tired of you

I thought I'd never
grow tired of you.

I thought I'd always
spend my life needing you.

I thought I'd never
grow this strong.

I thought I'd always
stay the child you found

but you made him
better than yourself.

don't leave, run

Run.

Don't leave.

Run.

Take it all with you.

Run.

Throw goodbye parties.

Run.

Always be there.

Run.

Don't leave.

Run.

grip

She gives out hugs
like you're headed off to War.
Squeezes like she'll never
see you again.

She knows how to
make you feel felt.

Reminding you,
at least in her grip,
you are wanted.

play things

We each have
our play things.
And instead of fight,
we covet being
the other's toy.

But we play so differently.
I want to play your game.
You just want to find it a nice home.

battle of age (so much older)

When you're young,
the *battle of age*
is all about experience.

"So much older."
It doesn't mean the calender.
Older is a sneaky shorthand
for having done 'more'.

Been more places.
Suffered more.
Lived more.
Some people live
a decade in a month.

Eventually,
only your parents
are older than you.

Run to them,
ask how they did it.

They'll say they
don't remember.
It was so long ago,
but they made it through.

That's all they
know for certain.
They made it.
And you will too.

wordsmiths

My eyes only saw characters.
If they're real, I couldn't tell.
The stories of their lives
were unwritten manuscripts.

All we ever did was
write and re-write stories.

So now,
and not for the first time,
I'll re-write ours, and
eventually,
you'll do the same.

We're wordsmiths, you and I.
So great that we have
the awful privilege of
writing our own pasts.

Part Five - Tomorrows

west

Aiming west
on the road,
the things behind
lie ahead
because they
come with you.

some have god

You can see out my eyes,
I just know it.

Watching me somewhere
far from here.

You tune in, watching
and judging blindly.

I can feel your eyes peering,
dissecting my day.

While some have god,
I have you.

go quiet

Being alone can only
hurt when you go quiet.

The voices, the strings,
the tones, the hums.

When the artificial
sounds become as
warm as the natural lights,

it can suddenly feel like
old friends are around,
flickering again.

metal accents

Bare toes on metal accents.
Skin cool in the warmth
of velvet and wood.

Silver-gold bars,
beams made to look
sophisticated,
cooling my feet in
the most primal and
natural way.

the goddess of the hearth

The Goddess of the Hearth
is here with she and I.
The tender threesome
of heat and dirt
wrapping us in
soft and sore stones.
That timeless voice echoing
from her lips instead,
full and love

doomsday

The problem with Doomsday cults
is they're always disappointed.

Preparing, preserving,
purifying, preaching.

But the only end
they witness is their own,
and not for very long.

The key is to
get that all out of your
system when you're young.

So when that Doomsday comes,
you're already used to it.

layers II

And the day I come to you
stripped of my layers,
a tank top and shorts
clung to my disagreeable frame,
you'll know my summer has arrived.

idols

My idols aren't prophets,
heroes, or talents.

They're hurt, glamorous,
deeply self aware people
trying their best.

That's what I strive
to be - any part of it.

(Save hurt, of course)

rhyming is flashy

Rhyming is flashy.
Emily makes it look easy.

Alliteration is cheap.
Anyone with a dictionary
can pull that one off.

Pain breeds poetry.
Enough pain to feel,
not enough to keep
from writing it down.

deal with tomorrow

Oh, I can deal with
myself tomorrow.

By the time I get to them —
myself and tomorrow —
we'll be one and the same.

Not then,
not them,
but me.

Thank you to everyone who helped get me started.

Instagram: @inside_pocket_poetry

Lightning Source UK Ltd.
Milton Keynes UK
UKHW040725060323
418105UK00002B/452